NATIONAL GEOGRAPHIC

A Pride of Lions

Rachel Griffiths and Margaret Clyne

Lions live in a group.
A group of lions is called a **pride**.

Count the lions in the pride.

Sheep live in a group.
A group of sheep is called a flock.

Count the sheep in the flock.

Kangaroos live in a group.
A group of kangaroos is called a **mob**.

Count the kangaroos in the mob.

Geese live in a group.
A group of geese is called a **gaggle**.

Count the geese in the gaggle.

Bison live in a group.
A group of bison is called a **herd**.

Count the bison in the herd.

Glossary

flock of sheep

gaggle of geese

herd of bison

mob of kangaroos

pride of lions